Financial Management Service

U.S. Department of the Treasury

**Strategic Plan
FY 2008 – 2013**

June 2008

The Financial Management Service (FMS) is the federal government's financial manager. We provide central payment services to agencies, operate the government's collections systems, provide government-wide accounting and reporting, and collect delinquent debt. It is a critical mission for which we must thoroughly plan and professionally execute. This strategic plan builds on our outstanding record of past performance and lays out our goals and strategies for the future.

The work we do every day touches millions of American citizens and virtually every federal agency. Our collections programs efficiently collect the monies the government needs to provide for our national defense, social and educational programs, medical research, and more. Government-wide accounting provides the daily, monthly and annual financial information needed for economic and investment decisions. Our payments operations ensure that people get the benefits dollars needed to pay the rent and buy food and they can count on receiving those payments on time, every time. And, our Debt Management operations collects debt owed to the government that otherwise would go unrecovered, including delinquent child support that is returned to custodial parents to raise American children.

As Commissioner, I am passionate about our mission and proud of the FMS employees, contractors, and fiscal and financial agents that share that passion and deliver quality service every day. This strategic plan keeps us focused on the goals, strategies, priorities and values that will ensure a future that positions FMS as a strong leader within and outside of the Federal sector.

You'll notice this strategic plan adds a goal: Be a great place to work. There is a Chinese proverb that says "If you want to plan for a year, grow rice; a decade, grow trees; a generation, grow people." FMS is committed to being a place where all employees are engaged, developed and valued.

We have done the planning. The goals are clear. Our values provide the foundation. It is time to act.

Sincerely,

Judith R. Tillman

Table of Contents

The Financial Management Service (FMS) is a bureau of the United States Department of the Treasury. FMS performs many of the fundamental cash management functions that were delegated to Treasury when Congress created the Department in 1789.

The Financial Management Service (FMS) plays a key role in supporting the Department of the Treasury's strategic goal of managing the United States Government's finances effectively by operating as the financial manager and principal fiscal agent for the Federal Government. This role includes managing the nation's finances by collecting money due to the United States (including delinquent debt), making its payments and performing central accounting functions.

FMS' workforce is comprised of over 1,900 people in the Washington, D.C. metropolitan area, four Regional Financial Centers located in Austin, Texas; Kansas City, Missouri; Philadelphia, Pennsylvania; San Francisco, California, and a Debt Management Operations Center.

For a detailed description of FMS' organizational structure, please see Appendix A.

Vision

World class delivery of Government financial management services

The Financial Management Service (FMS) will continue its vision of world class financial services while building on best-in-class processes, and a culture that embraces its core values.

Mission

To provide central payment services to Federal Program Agencies (FPAs), operate the Federal Government's collections and deposit systems, provide government-wide accounting and reporting services, and manage the collection of delinquent debt owed to the Government.

FMS provides critical services to millions of United States taxpayers and other customers. It embodies Treasury's leadership strategy to create value for the American people, provide responsible and effective stewardship over the government's finances, and focus on quality service, results and innovation. The breadth and scope of FMS' programs is enormous. Likewise, the impact of its programs on the economy and the American public is significant. FMS' activities touch millions of American citizens, virtually every Federal Program Agency (FPA) and state governments across the country, as well as having international reach.

Three FMS programs – payments, collections and cash reporting – are part of the Nation's Financial Critical Infrastructure which requires these activities to be fully operational at all times.

Core Values

FMS strongly believes in a values-based culture. FMS' values are incorporated into all its activities and are captured by the principles of "Five I's":

- ***Information Sharing*** – Inform employees for better understanding of the overall environment and priorities.

- ***Inclusion*** – Give all employees the opportunity to fully use their talents and knowledge to help achieve quality results.

- ***Individual Respect*** – Value everyone's contributions and treat people right.

- ***Integrity*** – Promote a work environment with the highest ethical standards of honesty, trust and reliability. Ensuring integrity of data and systems is also part of this culture.

- ***Informality*** – Encourage openness and ease of communication.

Priorities

In support of the critical mission, FMS has established six overarching priorities that enable a positive and strong work environment.

Daily Operations – Delivering quality products and services in a timely manner.

Conversion from paper to electronics – Expanding and promoting the use of electronic media, moving towards an "all electronic Treasury".

Security of people, data, dollars, and physical locations – Ensuring safety of employees, the privacy of data, and the security of funds.

Cost management – Creating an efficient, optimal processing environment.

Operating by our values – Fostering an environment where core values are embraced.

Being a great place to work – Creating a positive work environment.

Goal 1
Timely, accurate and efficient disbursement of Federal payments.

Goal 2
Timely, accurate and efficient collection of Federal Government receipts.

Goal 3
Maximize collection of delinquent debt owed to the Government.

Goal 4
Timely and accurate financial information that contributes to the improved quality of financial decision making.

Goal 5
Be a great place to work.

Timely, accurate and efficient disbursement of Federal payments

The Financial Management Service (FMS) is the Government's central disbursing agency, issuing 85% of all payments on behalf of Federal Program Agencies (FPAs). FMS develops and implements Federal payment policy and procedures, promotes the use of electronics in the payment process, and assists agencies in converting payments from paper checks to Electronic Fund Transfer (EFT). This includes controlling and providing financial integrity to the payments process through reconciliation, accounting and claims activities.

Strategies

The following strategies are used to achieve this goal:

- **Maintain an optimal, secure payment processing environment.**

FMS is continually striving to achieve the optimal payment processing environment, while ensuring payments are processed at the highest level of security. Given its critical role in disbursing payments, FMS will continue to provide absolute assurance of the continuity of its operations.

The optimal payment processing environment is convenient, efficient, cost effective, and secure for both the Federal payment recipient and the initiating Federal agency.

- **Promote and expand the use of electronic media to deliver Federal payments.**

FMS will continue to concentrate its efforts on expanding and marketing the use of electronic media to deliver Federal payments. These efforts, such as nationwide campaigns to promote direct deposit and debit cards for unbanked, educate and encourage current check recipients to switch to electronic payment. Electronic media provide a safer, more secure and reliable method of payment. They also decrease the number of paper checks issued, which minimizes costs and inefficiencies associated with the delivery of non-electronic payments.

- **Expand outreach to customers to improve business processes.**

FMS will continue to work collaboratively with its customers, especially Federal Program Agencies, to improve business processes. For example, FMS works closely with the Social Security Administration to seek ways to improve the services we provide. An estimated four million social security and supplemental social security recipients do not have bank accounts, and therefore receive paper checks. FMS has introduced a prepaid debit card to deliver federal benefits to recipients who do not have a bank account. A debit card offers a safe, convenient, low cost electronic alternative for unbanked federal benefit check recipients to receive electronic fund transfer.

- **Streamline and modernize payment processes to move towards more efficient, cost effective payment platforms.**

Streamlining the payments process while continually investing in state-of-the-art technology is integral in processing payments accurately, timely, safely and securely to taxpayers.

FMS has undertaken considerable efforts to modernize its payment systems through the incorporation of new technologies and the internet. FMS has undertaken efforts to modernize the current mainframe-based software applications that are used to disburse approximately one billion Federal payments worth over $1.5 trillion annually. FMS is also developing an internet application that will provide a centralized electronic invoicing and payment information portal accessible to all participants in Federal payment transactions: agencies, payment recipients, and FMS.

Modernizing FMS' systems not only lowers costs for FMS, but provides governmentwide savings by streamlining functions and processes for all agencies.

- **Provide customers with an accurate, secure and convenient way to receive Federal payments.**

FMS will continue to provide its customers with best in class service and enhance its web-based programs. For example, FMS now provides an electronic office environment for check activities, including the reconciliation of more than 220 million check payments and the processing of over 1.5 million claims inquiries per year. Agencies are now able to access both check and automated clearinghouse payment information in the same system.

FMS continues to refine the process by which organizations (including states, universities, for-profit and non-profit entities) receive Federal funds from accounts pre-authorized by Federal agencies through an electronic grants payment system, making the payments quicker and safer. In addition, FMS will continue to promote electronic media for international payments.

FMS' *Stored Value Card (SVC)* has a direct benefit for our military, including troops fighting overseas. The SVC is a smartcard, similar to a credit/debit card, using an encrypted computer chip to process "electronic money" stored on the card. These cards are given to military members overseas with an aim at reducing the float-loss associated with more than $2 billion in coin and currency in circulation at military bases, ships at sea, and other closed government locations around the world.

FMS is working with the Department of Defense to develop a strategy to consolidate the three distinct military SVC programs currently managed by two Treasury agents into a single, multi-function enterprise-wide application, which will continue to meet the varied needs of each military organization utilizing the program. In addition, FMS is in the early stages of assessing the potential benefits and implications of using other technology to support electronic payments/funds transfer, for example, mobile phone technology.

Key Factors that Could Affect Achievement of the Strategic Goal

- *The willingness of unbanked federal check recipients to convert to EFT. FMS is constantly working on increasing the use and acceptance of debit cards by unbanked federal check recipients as benefit payment mechanism.*
- *The ability of agencies to successfully encourage payment recipients to use available EFT tools. FMS partners with the agencies to promote the use of direct deposit and debit cards for unbanked and educate payment recipients on the use of these available EFT tools.*

Timely, accurate and efficient collection of Federal Government receipts

The Financial Management Service (FMS) is responsible for administering the world's largest collections program. FMS collects revenues needed to operate the Federal Government through the effective management of the Government's collections infrastructure. The Federal Government's collection activities center around three major groups: (1) individuals, (2) businesses/ financial institutions, and (3) other Federal entities.

FMS develops and implements collections policies and procedures for the Federal Government, facilitates efficient collections by designing and administering state-of-the art collection systems, and promotes electronic collections to Federal Program Agencies (FPAs).

Strategies

The following strategies are used to achieve this goal:

- **Develop an optimal, secure revenue collection environment.**

FMS strives to achieve the optimal revenue collection environment, while ensuring collections are processed at the highest level of security. This environment is developed and operated in cooperation with fiscal and financial agents across the country and throughout the world. FMS will continue to promote the use of electronics in the collections process and assist agencies in converting collections from paper to electronic media to provide the most convenient, efficient, cost effective, and secure collection environment. This environment will be flexible enough to accommodate the varying needs and technical sophistication of all taxpayers and FPAs.

- **Promote and expand the use of electronic media to collect Federal receipts.**

FMS will continue to expand the use of electronic collection mechanisms that use the most advanced and secure collection technologies. Approximately 80 percent of the dollar volume of collections is processed electronically, while only 50 percent of the transactions are electronic.

FMS' *Electronic Federal Tax Payment System (EFTPS)* is the largest tax collection system in the world. It offers all businesses and individuals the convenience of making their Federal tax payments electronically 24 hours a day, 7 days a week. This system provides an accurate, secure and convenient way to pay Federal taxes. FMS will continue to communicate the benefits of the EFTPS – accuracy, security, simplicity and flexibility – to financial institutions, small businesses and tax practitioners. The goal is to encourage businesses and individuals to pay their Federal taxes electronically through EFTPS rather than by using paper Federal Tax Deposit (FTD) coupons.

FMS will also continue to promote Pay.gov, an innovative system that allows individuals and businesses to make non-tax payments to Federal agencies over the internet 24 hours a day, 7 days a week.

- **Expand outreach efforts and provide incentives to increase electronic collections to improve business processes.**

FMS is implementing a holistic approach with FPAs to improve cash management practices governmentwide. The goal is to establish a management framework for moving toward an all-electronic Treasury.

FMS will work closely with FPAs to develop a complete understanding of an FPA's entire collection portfolio and will recommend an integrated set of mechanisms to meet an agency's collection needs. FMS will also establish relationships in the Chief Financial Officer's (CFO's) office to develop and administer the agency-wide holistic approach, rather than working with an agency on an individual program or ad hoc request basis.

- **Streamline and modernize collections processes to move towards more efficient, cost effective collection mechanisms.**

FMS initiated a major new effort to streamline and modernize FMS' and Treasury's collections and cash management programs. This initiative will improve financial performance by enabling FMS and Government agencies to more effectively manage financial transaction information and improve the efficiency of the collections information reporting processes. It will also reduce the number of collections and cash management systems and processes and eliminate the duplication of data, products, interfaces, and technologies. This effort will simplify and standardize systems and processes that have accumulated over 30 years.

- **Provide customers with an accurate, secure and convenient way to process collections.**

FMS will continue to provide its customers with best in class service through the improvement and enhancement of its collections settlement services and programs. Through the use of these services/programs, FMS enables the conversion of a paper check either into an image that is cleared through the banking system or into an EFT debit against the check writer's bank account. In both cases, paper checks are digitized at the point of receipt and the transactions are cleared and settled electronically.

FMS will also continue to focus on security oversight efforts at financial agent processing facilities and banking institutions as a way to proactively identify security control weaknesses and detect and deter fraud, waste, theft and unauthorized access associated with the collection of government remittances and protection of sensitive information.

Key Factors that Could Affect Achievement of the Strategic Goal

- *Coordination with key stakeholders, the small business community, and tax professionals to convert major tax payment types to EFT.*
- *Competing program priorities and resources of Federal agencies and other FMS government-wide initiatives that conflict with the timing for EFT conversion efforts.*

Maximize collection of delinquent debt owed to the Government

The Debt Collection Improvement Act (DCIA) of 1996 and related legislation provide the tools for administering a centralized program for the collection of delinquent non-tax debts owed to the Federal Government. The Financial Management Service (FMS) serves as the government's central administrative debt collection agency. FMS also collects delinquent child support debts and delinquent state income tax debts, and assists the Internal Revenue Service (IRS) with the collection of delinquent taxes. FMS provides oversight and operational services to Federal Program Agencies (FPAs) and states as required by law.

Strategies

The following strategies are used to achieve this goal:

- **Pursue strategic alliances with FMS' partners to develop innovative debt collection tools.**

FMS works closely with both the public and private sector to search for new ways to increase the referral and collection of delinquent debt. Specifically, FMS has worked closely with IRS to make significant changes in the administration of the tax levy program, resulting in increased collections of delinquent federal taxes. FMS will continue to incorporate additional payment types into the payment offset and levy programs. These efforts increase the collection of debt, especially tax debt owed by contractors and vendors.

- **Propose legislation to increase and enhance debt collection opportunities.**

FMS has issued numerous regulations on debt collection and will continue to propose legislation to simplify and improve FMS' efforts in debt collection. Through new legislation, FMS allows its partners to effectively use the debt collection programs, maximize revenue and shift the cost of enforcement to delinquent tax debtors.

- **Seek new collection tools and initiatives to incorporate additional payment streams and debts.**

FMS collects delinquent debt through many tools and programs, including, but not limited to, the Cross-Servicing Program and the Treasury Offset Program (TOP). Cross-Servicing is the process whereby federal agencies refer delinquent debts to Treasury for collection. The Treasury Offset Program is a centralized offset program, administered by FMS, to collect delinquent debts owed to federal agencies and states (including past-due child support).

FMS will continue to expand the offset program to maximize delinquent debt collection through the incorporation of additional payments and debts.

- **Strengthen debt collection/management systems' security and functionality to provide agencies with secure and effortless use.**

The security of FMS' debt collection systems is paramount to FMS' delinquent debt program. Through systems such as *FedDebt*, a comprehensive system that integrates FMS' Cross-Servicing and Treasury Offset Programs, FMS ensures that its customers receive efficient and secure service. FedDebt provides Federal agency users with a Web-based interface to FMS' debt collection system. This system has the capacity to separate and protect sensitive data (Personally Identifiable Information) and employs stringent user authentication procedures, protecting the financial interests of the American taxpayer.

FMS will continue developing FedDebt by implementing a service-oriented architecture and enhancing the security and usability of the system as new technologies become available.

- **Seek new technologies to streamline, modernize and improve business processes and systems.**

FMS, through its debt collection program, will continue to improve the quality of the Federal Government's financial management by increasing the collection of delinquent debt owed to the Government, providing debt management services to all Federal agencies, and protecting the financial interests of the American taxpayer. In addition, FMS will continually assess its systems and processes as new technologies become available in search of ways to streamline processes and increase efficiencies through modernization.

- **Provide expert consulting services to agencies, to better assist them with determining debt management tools to increase collections while decreasing agency burden, through increased communication and collaboration.**

FMS will enhance communication and collaboration with Federal, State, and local agencies regarding their implementation and/or increased use of collection tools. These tools include *Administrative Wage Garnishment* (AWG), which allows private collection agencies to garnish private sector wages of delinquent debtors to collect agency debts, and *Debt Check* (an online database), which assist agencies in barring delinquent debtors from obtaining new Government loans or loan guarantees.

Key Factors that Could Affect Achievement of the Strategic Goal

- *The ability of agencies to refer debts to FMS for offset and cross-servicing, and for States to participate in administrative offset under the State Tax Debt Program.*
- *The accuracy and reliability of agency debt collection systems and records to ensure that referred debts are valid and legally enforceable.*
- *Unique statutory constraints on certain agencies.*

Timely and accurate financial information that contributes to the improved quality of financial decision making

The Financial Management Service (FMS) provides financial accounting and reporting services for the U.S. Government. FMS maintains the Federal Government's books and accounts for its monetary assets and liabilities by operating and overseeing the Government's central accounting and reporting system. It also works with Federal agencies to adopt uniform accounting and reporting standards and systems. FMS provides support, guidance and training to assist Federal Program Agencies (FPAs) in improving their government-wide accounting and reporting responsibilities.

FMS is responsible for gathering and publishing the government-wide financial information that is used by the public and private sectors to monitor the Government's financial status. These publications include: the Daily Treasury Statement, the Monthly Treasury Statement, the Treasury Bulletin, the Combined Statement of the United States Government, and the Financial Report of the United States Government (FR).

Strategies

The following strategies are used to achieve this goal:

- **Increase program efficiencies by reducing reporting burdens.**

Through programs such as FMS' Government-Wide Accounting (GWA) Modernization Project, FMS will improve the reliability, usefulness, and timeliness of the Government's financial information. In addition, FMS will provide agencies and other users with better access to financial information and eliminate duplicate reporting and reconciliation burdens. FMS will work with FPAs to report payment, collection and intra-governmental payment and collection transactions to the new GWA system.

- **Provide earlier and easier access to more useful and reliable information.**

FMS will continue to place increased emphasis on improving the quality, timeliness and integrity of the Federal Government's financial data. FMS will continue to revamp and implement government-wide accounting processes to provide more useful and reliable financial information on a regular basis.

FMS is redesigning its systems to provide agencies with daily direct access to financial information through a web-based system. This will allow customers to obtain fund balance information on the day after a transaction, giving decision makers more useful and timely information.

- **Provide agencies with secure access to FMS' systems and information.**

FMS will continue efforts to keep the financial systems and information accessible to legitimate users. FMS will continue to ensure, through its systems and initiatives, greater accuracy, integrity, and security of government-wide financial information.

- **Expand outreach to customers to improve business processes.**

FMS will continue to work with outside agencies to improve government-wide accounting and reporting. FMS will continue to use the Chief Financial Officers (CFO) Council, Treasury Reporting Group as a forum to discuss accounting and reporting issues that affect the Financial Report. FMS will continue to work with the CFO Council and the Office of Management and Budget (OMB) to develop more consistent business rules for intra-governmental transactions.

- **Provide tools and methodologies to improve accuracy, integrity and consistency of financial data.**

FMS will continue to modernize long standing federal accounting processes, and provide agencies with methodologies and tools to improve the accuracy and consistency of their financial data. Through these methodologies and tools, FMS will improve the exchange of financial information among FMS, FPAs, OMB and the banking community, and will comprehensively replace current government-wide accounting functions and processes that are both internal and external to FMS.

FMS will also integrate budget and financial reports from FPAs, and improve the consistency of the budgetary and proprietary accounting data recorded in agency financial statements and reported to FMS through its trial balance.

- **Provide agencies and other concerned parties with financial management and accounting guidelines, and regulations.**

FMS will continue to establish standardized government-wide accounts, transactions and accounting entries, for new and updated Federal Accounting Standards Advisory Board (FASAB) and OMB accounting and reporting policy and accounting standards.

FMS issues the Treasury Financial Manual (TFM) to provide policies, procedures, and instructions for Federal departments and agencies, Federal Reserve Banks (FRBs), and other concerned parties. The TFM is Treasury's official guidance for financial accounting and reporting of all receipts and disbursements of the Federal Government. Sections of this manual are updated periodically by FMS, as new regulations and procedures arise.

17

- **Strengthen and improve the quality and reporting of financial information of the U.S. Government.**

FMS will continue to take significant actions to address the material weaknesses found in the compilation process of the Financial Report (FR) of the United States Government. The goal of these actions is to remove the weaknesses found in compiling the FR as a barrier to get a clean audit opinion.

Key Factors that Could Affect Achievement of the Strategic Goal

- *FMS relies on the FPAs, financial institutions, and the FRBs to report to FMS the underlying transactions necessary to accomplish its responsibilities. Changes made by FMS to improve overall reporting will, most likely, require changes in the systems and processes of these organizations.*

- *FMS relies on FPA information for preparing and publishing the Financial Report of the U. S. Government. Our success in addressing areas that FMS has taken the lead to resolve is dependent on the quality and timeliness of program agency financial reporting. Improvements made by FMS in the processes for preparing and reporting governmentwide financial statements will most likely affect changes in program agency systems and processes.*

Be a great place to work

The Financial Management Service (FMS) strives to maintain a positive work environment, where employees feel engaged and where achievement is valued. FMS encourages employees to apply their talent, skills and knowledge to the fullest in ways enabling them to consistently deliver excellence in products and services.

FMS continues to demonstrate its commitment to diversity by accepting and recognizing the contributions of all employees and by understanding the strengths that arise from the broad range of backgrounds, cultures, customs, and beliefs.

Our organizational values of ***Information Sharing, Inclusion, Individual Respect, Integrity and Informality*** (the Five I's at FMS), provide a foundation for our service delivery. We work to foster an environmental culture of quality awareness that encourages all employees to continuously look for ways to improve accuracy, timeliness and customer service.

In support of its mission, FMS builds a workforce that is citizen-centered, results-oriented, and mission-focused. FMS works to implement initiatives and programs that will deliver results and provide quality service to millions of citizens.

FMS continuously works to improve the quality of its professional workforce. FMS' Human Capital Strategic Plan identifies the agency's approach to addressing its human capital challenges.

Strategies

The following strategies are used to achieve this goal:

- **Provide developmental opportunities to employees.**

FMS is committed to developing and retaining a well-trained, high-performing, diverse workforce that effectively meets changing mission requirements and program priorities.

FMS is committed to providing ongoing training of all its employees. FMS has developed a centralized system of training and development available for employees at all levels which includes training in specific job skill areas as well as computer skills, administration, management, and career decisional subjects.

FMS continues to support and provide the best opportunities for achievement and learning. FMS values learning and development and provides a motivational environment for employees to grow their skills and knowledge.

- **Train managers and provide tools to cultivate the best leaders.**

FMS recognizes management as a unique profession with its own specialized skills, challenges and levels of expertise. FMS has identified and implemented a set of core management knowledge, skills and abilities an FMS leader or manager should have to achieve significant performance.

FMS will continue to provide structured management and executive development programs to help employees succeed in management positions. These programs ensure continuity of leadership, and sustain a learning environment.

- **Communicate effectively with all employees.**

Open communication is a key value at FMS. FMS continues to build and expand on its communication systems and practices which results in a more knowledgeable and highly motivated workforce. FMS has several communication vehicles such as monthly media magazines, informal memoranda to all employees, an informative intranet site and information sharing meetings.

In addition to surveys conducted by the Office of Personnel and Management (OPM), FMS conducts periodic surveys to obtain the employees perspective on the organization, and incorporates the results of these surveys in the organization's management goals.

- **Operate by our established values.**

FMS has identified five principles as values: Information Sharing, Inclusion, Individual Respect, Integrity, Informality and Innovation. Through our actions and the quality delivery of our products and services, FMS demonstrates these values. FMS provides employees with flexibility and support to achieve a work-life balance and quality.

FMS fosters a participative environment where employees are involved in decision-making related to their work, job and career. By working in an all inclusive, information sharing and informal environment, employees feel their opinions are valued and therefore are highly motivated to produce excellence.

- **Maintain a safe and secure work environment.**

Keeping FMS' workforce safe is a top priority. Given the nature of FMS' work, FMS has taken every effort to ensure that its employees at both its headquarters and regional centers are safe and secure. FMS always seeks to identify challenges and solutions to improve the safety of employees and their work.

Key Factors that Could Affect Achievement of the Strategic Goal

- *Recruitment challenges in attracting highly skilled workforce.*
- *Developing and retaining current employees.*
- *Effectively competing for skilled employees with the private sector.*

Appendix A: Financial Management Service Organizations

The Financial Management Service (FMS) is comprised of a Commissioner's Office and six major Assistant Commissioner Areas: Debt Management Services, Federal Finance, Governmentwide Accounting, Information Resources, Management, and Payment Management organized to accomplish its mission.

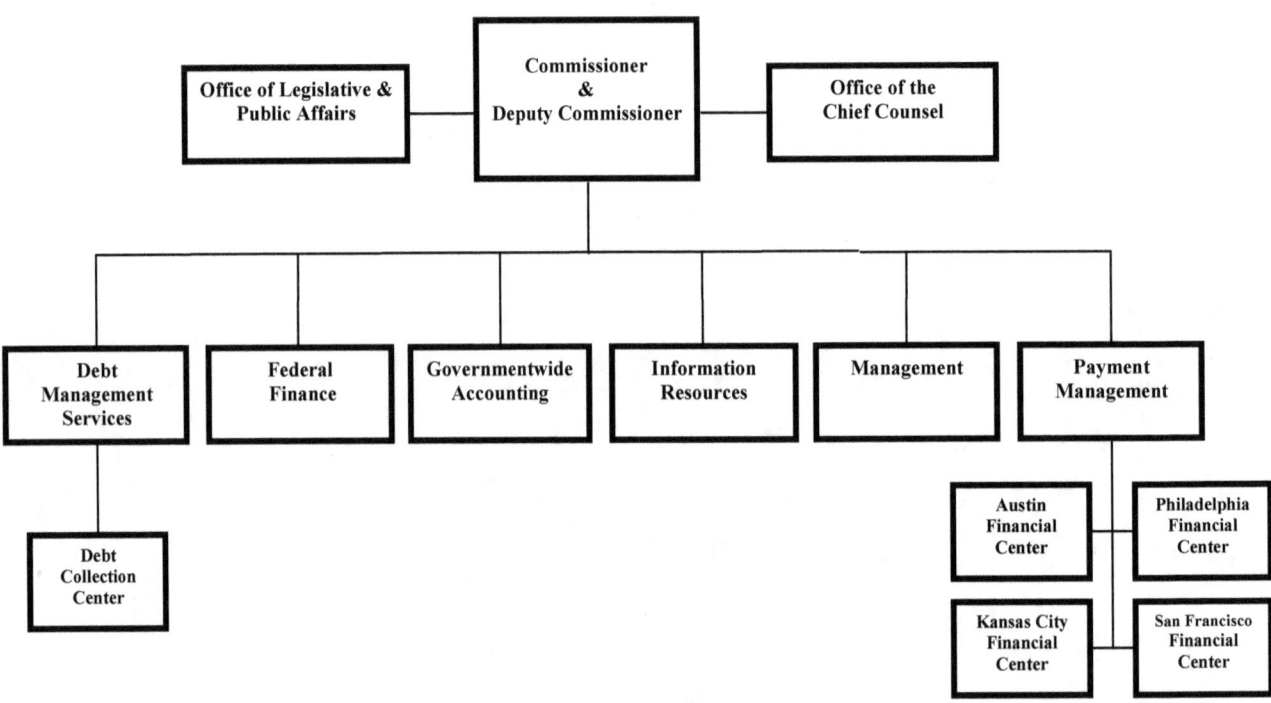

Office of the Commissioner
The Office of the Commissioner includes the Office of the Chief Counsel, the Office of Legislative and Public Affairs, and the Federal Reserve Bank (FRB) Liaison. The Office of the Chief Counsel provides legal counsel and advice to support the Financial Management Service in all aspects of its mission, including program and policy initiatives as well as general administrative activities. The Office of Legislative and Public Affairs serves as the FMS' liaison with Congress, the news media and the public.

Assistant Commissioner Areas

Debt Management Services
Debt Management Services' (DMS) Assistant Commissioner area's primary focus is to improve the quality of the Federal Government's financial management by increasing the collection of delinquent debt owed to the Government, by providing debt management services to all Federal agencies, and by protecting the financial interests of the American taxpayer. DMS also develops and implements governmentwide debt management policies.

Federal Finance
Federal Finance's (FF) Assistant Commissioner area's primary focus is to evaluate, develop and operate collection and cash management programs that minimize cost and maximize the effectiveness and efficiency of Federal Government's financial management.

Governmentwide Accounting
Governmentwide Accounting (GWA) Assistant Commissioner area's primary focus is to provide the financial infrastructure for Federal central accounting and governmentwide reporting, reconcile agency and bank reporting differences, and generate the Daily Treasury Statement (DTS), Monthly Treasury Statement (MTS), and quarterly financial reports. In addition, Governmentwide Accounting is responsible for the annual compilation and publication of the Financial Report (FR) of the United States Government.

Information Resources
Information Resources' (IR) Assistant Commissioner area's primary focus is to direct and support all aspects of FMS' technology and information systems, and ensure the effective use of information technology throughout FMS.

Management
The Management Assistant Commissioner area's primary focus is to provide direction and leadership for FMS' administrative and financial programs, ensuring that policies developed and implemented for resource management conform to Federal and Departmental regulatory requirements. Management is FMS' primary checkpoint for administrative services - from procurements to personnel actions, from building services to security.

Payment Management

Payment Management (PM) Assistant Commissioner area's primary focus is to manage and operate Federal disbursement and related aftermath systems. PM is headquartered in Washington, DC and Hyattsville, MD and supported by four regional financial centers located in: Austin, TX; Kansas City, MO; Philadelphia, PA; and San Francisco, CA. PM disburses an enormous volume of payments and associated dollars that represents approximately 85% of all Federal payments issued. PM also handles payment aftermath functions that include researching claims of non-receipt, processing returns, handling reclamation requests, and performing related accounting functions.

Appendix B: Linkage Between Treasury Department Goals & Objectives and FMS' Goals

The FMS implementation of Government Performance and Results Act (GPRA) links the FMS Strategic Plan, the Annual Performance Plans and Reports, and the budget. Our performance goals in the Budget/Annual Plans and Reports are identical to our strategic goals in the strategic plan.

Treasury Goals and Objectives	FMS Goals
Goal: *Effectively Managed U.S. Government Finances*	
Objective: ■ Cash resources are available to operate the government	**Goal 1:** Timely, accurate and efficient disbursement of federal payments.
Strategies: ■ Optimize cash and debt portfolio	**Goal 2:** Timely, accurate and efficient collection of federal government receipts.
■ Expand all-electronic transactions ■ Modernize	**Goal 3:** Maximize collection of delinquent debt owed to the government.
■ Standardize	**Goal 4:** Timely and accurate financial information that contributes to the improved quality of financial decision making.
Goal: *Management and Organizational Excellence*	
Objective: ■ Enabled and effective Treasury Department **Strategies:** ■ Communicate and collaborate effectively with Congress and other stakeholders ■ Align and optimize resources strategically ■ Invest in people & technology	**Goal 5:** Be a great place to work.

Appendix C: Linkage Between Treasury Department Value Chains & Outcomes and FMS' Goals

	Treasury	Financial Management service
Value Chains	**Outcomes**	**Strategic Goals**
Collect	*Revenue collected when due through a fair and uniform application of the law*	Timely, accurate and efficient collection of federal government receipts. Maximize collection of delinquent debt owed to the government.
Disburse	*Timely and accurate payments at the lowest possible cost*	Timely, accurate and efficient disbursement of federal payments.
Account	*Effective cash management* *Accurate, timely, useful, transparent and accessible financial information*	Timely and accurate financial information that contributes to the improved quality of financial decision making.
Manage	*A citizen-centered, results-oriented and strategically aligned organization* *Exceptional accountability and transparency*	Be a great place to work.

Appendix D: FMS Long-Term Strategic Performance Goals / Measures

The following long-term goals/measures support the major FMS mission activities. These goals/measures may be revised and/or changed as a result of business environment changes. The targets listed below are set for 2018.

Payments

Ninety percent of all payments will be made electronically

Collections

Ninety percent of the dollar amount of all collections will be made electronically

Debt Collection

There will be $8 billion dollars collected annually from delinquent debt referrals.

Governmentwide Accounting and Reporting

By 2018, there will be no material weaknesses in the FR as it relates to Treasury's systems, policies, and procedures used to collect and consolidate governmentwide financial information.

Appendix E: Key Factors Affecting All FMS' Strategic Goals

- **Budget Environment** - Tight fiscal constraints will drive FMS to continue leveraging its resources for maximum program efficiencies.

- **Reliance on other Government Agencies**– Given the breath and scope of FMS' mission, we are dependent on other Government agencies when implementing changes and in achieving our goals.

- **Technology** - FMS' systems must adapt to new technological advancements, including those in the area of electronic commerce and security. Also, as mentioned above, the optimal operation of FMS' systems is often dependant on other agencies' ability to adapt to these new technological advancements.

- **Human Capital** – Forces such as cultural attitudes and expectations, structural issues related to Federal employment, workforce demographics, and security concerns produce a human resources environment that is fluid, complex, and challenging.

  - **Future Skill Needs** - FMS' primary challenge is to successfully recruit and retain employees who fulfill our current occupational skill set.

  - **Workforce / Succession Planning** – The executive management team considers succession planning an integral part of its responsibilities. This consideration permeates much of the decision process relative to staffing and development.

Appendix F: Strategic Management Process

FMS' strategic management process reflects the vision of the Commissioner and the FMS senior management team and engages the executive level planning group in a continuous effort. This effort focuses on evaluating the nature of the business; articulating a futuristic vision for how FMS business will be conducted; defining long-term goals; developing realistic objectives and strategies to reach those goals; aligning those goals and objectives with our budget and with Department of the Treasury's Strategic Plan; establishing performance measures; and allocating resources appropriately to carry out the goals, objectives and strategies. This effort embodies inclusiveness and participation from FMS managers, employees, customers and stakeholders. Accountability for the strategic plan is two-fold: 1) tactical or action level plans that are in alignment with the strategic plan; and 2) Senior Executive Service Performance Plans.

Set strategic goals and priorities for the long-term. FMS' Strategic Plan sets goals and strategies to guide the entire organization. It also serves as the baseline for the development of tactical or action level plans, performance goals, annual plans, and budget initiatives. As with all other government agencies, FMS operates in an environment (e.g., political, economic, social) that is constantly changing. These changes may affect FMS' ability to meet its goals. As a result, FMS' Strategic Plan includes descriptions of the external factors that may affect our ability to achieve our goals.

Set annual performance targets. FMS has formatted its budget submission to serve as both a budget request and as the Government Performance and Results Act (GPRA) performance plan. The performance goals included in the budget submission drive program decision-making and serve to justify the resource request. We derive the performance goals and targets presented in the budget justification from the strategic goals presented in the strategic plan.

Manage and budget to achieve those targets. FMS links program results and budget activities to fulfill GPRA requirements. FMS has four budget activities that link functions to FMS' current performance measures and strategic goals: Payments, Collections, Debt Collection, and Governmentwide Accounting and Reporting. The budget activities represent the major activities that support the FMS mission.

Systematically report on annual performance. FMS' annual budget submission also includes the annual performance report required by GPRA. Annually, we compare actual performance with the estimated targets, and we provide explanations for the differences between planned and actual target levels.

Program Evaluations

A number of ongoing and one-time program evaluations/audits have influenced FMS goals and strategies. FMS accomplishes program evaluations through a variety of sources: internal reviews conducted by individual program offices; reviews conducted by FMS' Comptroller Directorate, Finance and Internal Control Division; reviews and audits performed by Treasury's Office of the Inspector General (OIG) and reviews conducted by the General Accounting Office (GAO).

FMS continuously reviews and evaluates its programs. Included in the review process are periodic and spot reviews related to lockbox operations, certification and accreditation of all information technology systems, and management annual assurances in compliance with the Federal Financial Integrity Act and the Federal Financial Management Improvement Act.

Appendix G: Consultations and Stakeholders

This Strategic Plan was developed in accordance with the provisions of the GPRA and OMB Circular A-11. We have shared our initial draft plan with the Department and OMB. Their views and comments are reflected in this draft. We have sent letters to various Congressional Committees, Federal Program Agencies, and the National Treasury Employees Union requesting their review of and comments about our draft plan; and made the plan available at the FMS web site at http://www.fms.treas.gov/strategicplan/index.html.

Our consultation efforts are summarized below:

Congressional Consultations	
Senate	**House**
Chairman, Senate Appropriations Committee	Chairman, House Appropriations Committee
Ranking Member, Senate Appropriations Committee	Ranking Member, House Appropriations Committee
Chairman, Senate Appropriations Financial Services and General Government Subcommittee	Chairman, House Appropriations Financial Service and General Government Subcommittee
Ranking Member, Senate Appropriations Financial Services and General Government Subcommittee	Ranking Member, House Appropriations Financial Service and General Government Subcommittee
Chairman, Senate Committee on Homeland Security and Governmental Affairs	Chairman, House Oversight and Government Reform Committee
Ranking Member, Senate Committee on Homeland Security and Governmental Affairs	Ranking Member, House Oversight and Government Reform Committee

Customers and Stakeholders	
Social Security Administration	Department of Veterans Affairs
Office of Personnel Management	United States Mint
The Alcohol and Tobacco Tax and Trade Bureau	Railroad Retirement Board
Department of Defense	Department of State
Internal Revenue Service	U.S. Department of Agriculture
Federal Reserve System	National Treasury Employees Union
U.S. Postal Service	Department of Homeland Security

www.ingramcontent.com/pod-product-compliance
Lightning Source LLC
Chambersburg PA
CBHW052025280526
45793CB00005B/1128